*For Marie-Therese Pirotta* – S.G.

*For the good people of Chapel Allerton* – S.A.

Text copyright © 2002 Sam Godwin
Illustrations copyright © 2002 Simone Abel
Volume copyright © 2002 Hodder Wayland

Series concept and design: Liz Black
Book design: Jane Hawkins
Editor: Katie Orchard
Science Consultant: Dr Carol Ballard

Published in Great Britain in 2002 by Hodder Wayland,
an imprint of Hodder Children's Books

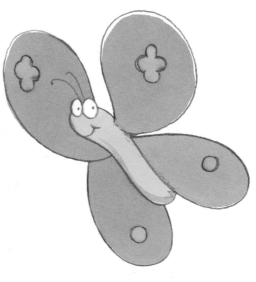

Cataloguing in publication data
Godwin, Sam
    It All Makes Sense: a first look at the senses – (Little Bees)
    1. Senses and sensation – Pictorial works – Juvenile literature
    I. Title
    612.8

ISBN 07502 3931 X

Printed and bound in Grafiasa, Porto, Portugal

Hodder Children's Books
A division of Hodder Headline Limited
338 Euston Road, London NW1 3BH

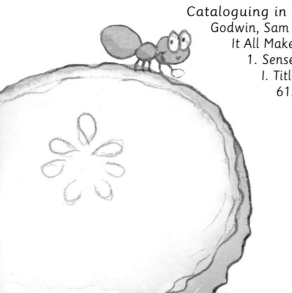
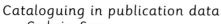

# It All Makes Sense!

## A first look at the senses

buzzᶻᶻ

# It All Makes Sense!

## A first look at the senses

### Sam Godwin

an imprint of Hodder Children's Books

12

from loud, clanging noises...

Ding Dong! ding dong!

It didn't make me happy. It woke me up!

Zzzz...

13

I can smell some tasty nectar.

Leave some for us!

Some things smell nice...

Don't touch it, dear. Some smelly things are full of germs!

19

And some taste sweet, or salty.

23

We can feel the world around us by touch.

Stone is very hard to sit on!

And some things feel cold or warm.

Brrr! This water feels very cold.

26

# All about the senses

We use all our senses at once when we eat an apple:

We see the bright colour of the apple.

We feel the smooth skin with our fingers.

We taste the sweet flavour of the apple.

We smell the aroma as we peel the apple.

# Useful Words

## Aroma
A pleasant smell.

## Bitter
A sharp, strong taste.

## Nectar
A sugary substance made by plants to attract insects. Bees make honey from it.

## Sour
An acid taste, like lemon or vinegar.

We hear ourselves chewing as we eat the apple. Yum, yum!